Momma Sayings

and Life Reflections

by
Lori M. Hobson

Finding your beauty

Finding Your Beauty Publishing

Finding your beauty

Third Edition

ISBN:
978-0-9818350-1-3

Cover design by
Shari Wilson
www.sharirocks.com

MOMMA SAYINGS DEDICATIONS

To my parents, my two biggest fans, the people who made me who I am and never lost sight of the things about me that are great, even when I did.

To my "big sister", Punkin, for proofing and making me laugh when I wanted to work and making me work when I wanted to laugh.

To my mentor and "other mother", Dr. Katie Davis; thank you for encouraging me to say who I am.

To my mentor, Carolyn Hines, thanks for your support and your firm hand.

To Jewel Diamond Taylor, "my sister from another mother." It was your challenge that moved *Momma Sayings* from the file on my computer to reality.

To my sisters, and all of my sister girls. You know who you are. I love you all for loving me.

To Gail, my "Anchor". You always know when I need you. I love you girl.

To my Wise Warren, thanks for keeping me fit.

To my beautiful Goddaughters, Ryanne and Kirstin, for teaching me so much and listening to my momma sayings. I don't simply love you. I adore you.

To TW3, it will be great when they call us all Doctor.

To Laverne "Momma" Espy. Thanks for always being there.

To my fellow master minds, "The Sensational Six", and Michelle, the world's best coach, thank you for having my back.

To my family, my church families and everyone who contributed to this book.

Thank you all.

WHO'S ON THE COVER

Thank you to these amazing, incredible men and women that shared not only their sayings with me but were gracious enough to allow me to share their protraits with you.

Pictured on the cover, from top left to right are:

Sandy Dumont
Dr. Katie Davis
Gail Glassmoyer

Pictured on the cover, next to title:

Juanita Hobson, my mother
Carole DeRouen

Pictured on the cover, from bottom left to right are:

Pastors Dorothy and Lawrence Govan
Four Generations, Mrs. Melva Threatt Walker (seated), daughter Carolyn Hines and granddaughter Kimberly Hines Bullock, and great granddaughters Symone & Olyvia Bullock
Cyril and Constance Jermin

CONTENTS

INTRODUCTION

Momma Sayings and Life Reflections 3rd Edition

Within a few days of the release of the second edition, I had heard the same request several times. Readers were asking me to tell the story behind some of the sayings. So, in response to popular demand, Momma Sayings became *Momma Sayings and Life Reflections*. This third edition has new sayings, new chapters, a new cover and a story for each chapter.

My work as a counselor often involves clinical issues, serious mental health problems and situational issues. However, sometimes my work as a counselor, especially in an educational setting or with young people, involves simple nurturing. As a college counselor, I jokingly tell students that I do "Momma" very well. As a result, I often have students come in to see me simply because their Momma isn't around. Most of the time, they won't admit this to me but I have learned that if I was using many Momma Sayings, then this was more of a nurturing session than a counseling session.

Many times, I would be talking to a young person who was trying to navigate life's minefields and I would remember what my parents said to me when I was having a similar experience. That is how *Momma Sayings* was born. I would say to the young person; "Let me tell you one of my momma sayings."

When I ran out of sayings from my own parents, I started making them up. Then I started writing them down and as I shared my idea with friends, they added their momma sayings to my list. Eventually my list became the idea for this book. Here it is. I hope it gives you the warm feeling that it gives me. Wherever you see a name, it is the name of the person who gave me the saying. It may have been originated by someone else. If you don't see a name then it came from me. If somebody you know says it too, it's just a coincidence.

For the purpose of this book, Momma doesn't only mean your mother. Momma could be your father, sister, brother, uncle, cousin, best friend... Anybody who made a comment that has stuck with you for life. The fact is many of my momma sayings came from men.

I have always considered parenting to be the hardest job on the planet and I admire people who raise healthy, whole children tremendously. In October 2002, I had an experience that showed me that I was right about how hard parenting is. My youngest Goddaughter came to live with me. Suddenly I was not only a parent, but a single parent. I was thrilled to have her with me and terrified that I would make some horrendous mistake that would ruin our lives. What I came to realize was that GOD is with us always and that as long as we have faith, we will be just fine. She is grown now and I am happy to say that we both survived the experience.

When you are a counselor in a college setting, your "babies" end up all over the country. It is to be hoped that some of them will pick up this book and remember hearing some of these sayings in my little office while eating a piece of hard candy out of my desk drawer. I love them all and I know that they will remember that.

The first and second editions of this book were blessed with more success than I ever imagined. The first edition was more of an experiment than anything else. I printed a limited amount of copies and sold them all in a week. The success of the first edition motivated me to add more sayings and create a second edition. That edition went through two printings.

Now, I hope you enjoy the next edition of Momma Sayings and Life Reflections. I have definitely enjoyed all the amazing people that I have met on this incredible journey.

信仰

js

Faith

FAITH

*"Faith is the most powerful of all
forces operating in humanity.
And, when you have it in depth,
nothing can get you down.
Nothing!"* Norman Vincent Peale

An excerpt from
Legacy of Prayer
by Jennifer Kennedy Dean

"We need to mentor our children in prayer and faith. We have to make them part of our journey of discovery. We have to quit shielding them from our own struggles—the ones they can handle within the context of their age and maturity level. I used to think that I should let my children see only my faith, never my fear or my doubt or my struggle.

Later I realized that they thought I never had struggles or doubts. I have found it more to their advantage to let them see the whole process. If I don't let my children in on the crucifixion, they won't see the resurrection. If I don't let them in on the battle, they won't see the victory. If I don't let them in on the need, they won't see the supply. I find that if I am open with them, they are likely to be open with me.

Now that they are almost adults, they often let me in on their crucifixion moments, and I have the privilege of praying them through those and seeing them develop into men after God's own heart."

Sara Dean

"Don't try to stay in a place that GOD is trying to take you out of." **Jean C. Bellamy**

"Go where GOD tells you to go. Do what GOD tells you to do and stop when GOD tells you to stop." **Pastor Lawrence Govan, Progressive Life Worship Center**

"A Setback is a setup for a comeback. GOD is the comeback King." **Pastor Dawn Harvey-Destiny, International Christian Center**

"If you feel like you are far away from GOD, remember it was you who moved."
"GOD's work done GOD's way will not lack GOD's support." **Pastor Jerome A. Barber, Sixth Mount Zion Baptist Temple**

"Hang on to GOD's coattail and he will pull you through anything." **Gail Glassmoyer**

"There is nothing so broken that GOD cannot fix it." **T. Hurley Johnson**

"My mind is blessed, my heart is at rest, I have peace in You and I always know what to do." **Djuana Daniel**

"I won't give up on you and you can't give up on you. (Billboard signed GOD.)"

"Faith it 'til you make it." **Jewel Diamond Taylor**

"It may be a good thing but is it a GOD thing?"
Minister Ivey McGregor

"God never closes a door without opening a window somewhere else." **Mary Szymkowiak**

"When you have a real relationship with GOD, he first shows you him; then he shows you yourself."
Minister Ivey McGregor
Be careful of those people who say that they were with GOD and he told them about what is wrong with you. It is possible that they are just trying to criticize you in the name of GOD.

"GOD woke me up this morning, clothed in my right mind. I didn't understand that until I thought I would lose my mind."
Pastor Jerome A. Barber, Sixth Mount Zion Baptist Temple

"Faith won't always take away your fear. Just make sure that fear never takes away your faith."

"I asked GOD to fix my problems and he said "I did fix them. I gave you resilience." **Pastor Dawn Harvey-Destiny, International Christian Center**

"It's not only what you know but more important who you know; Remember, God's not blind."
Ann Beete-Graham

"Nobody's no can compete with GOD's yes!"
Jentezen Franklin

"Everyone needs to have ones twos and threes in their lives." **Minister Ivey McGregor**
   Ones are the people you look up to. If you have too many ones, you will always be reaching up. You may never feel as if you measure up. Twos are the people who are just like you, your peers. They will keep you right where you are and help you make excuses for not improving yourself. Whatever you do don't be "two" heavy. Three's are the people who look up to you. It is important to be a mentor and role model but too many three's can make you think more of yourself than you should. That can also impede your growth.

"In order to face the day I pray for: Peace, Courage Balance and Focus."
   With peace I can find what I need, with courage I can face what I find, with balance I can do what GOD expects of me and with focus I can see the path before me. Those things, along with GOD's strength help me to handle whatever comes my way.

"A storm with Jesus is a whole lot better than a storm without Jesus." **Pastor Jerome A. Barber, Sixth Mount Zion Baptist Temple**

"It is never too late to become what you might have been." **Pastor Dawn Harvey-Destiny, International Christian Center**

"There is no order of difficulty in miracles."
Marianne Williamson

"I am blessed and resilient! When shift and challenges happen, I don't break. I bend like a palm tree. I am calm and covered by the peace of GOD. I am guided to the best steps of action. I will walk by faith and stay in the light. Prov. 6:23"
Jewel Diamond Taylor

"If you have a big God you will have little problems, and if you have a little God you will have big problems." **Dwight Bain**

"The Prayer of Jabez should come with a warning label."

The prayer of Jabez is a very small passage it one of the less popular books of the bible. It says. "And Jabez called on the GOD of Israel saying, 'Oh that You would bless me indeed and enlarge my territory, that Your hand would be with me, and that You would keep me from evil, that I would not cause pain!' So GOD granted him what he requested" (1 Chronicles 4:10 New King James version).

What an amazingly powerful little prayer. This story is a part of my personal testimony. Everyone who knows me well has heard this story. It is something that I share with everyone who will listen; usually beginning with the following statement. "I think the prayer of Jabez should have a warning label just like the ones on cigarettes and prescription medications. In my opinion, this story is the most important life reflection in this book.

Several years ago, I was at the Dollar Store standing in the book aisle. A man whom I had never seen before, and never saw again, walked up to me and another woman and said "you should buy this book. It is at the book store next door for $12.99 and we have it here for a dollar. It is a great book and you should buy it!"

I took the book down from the shelf and looked at it. It was The Prayer of Jabez by Bruce Wilkinson. At first, I thought it was a children's book. As I thumbed through the beautifully illustrated pages, I realized that it was not a children's book and it was about some kind of prayer. I thought, "Why not? It is only a dollar," and decided to buy it. I took it home and tossed it, unopened, on my night stand. I didn't think any more about it.

Weeks later, I found myself awake at 4am and unable to go back to sleep. I looked around for something to read, hoping to relax enough to get back to sleep and my eyes settled on the previously forgotten volume. Again I thought "why not" and I picked it up. I ended up awake much longer because I couldn't put it down.

Bruce introduced a different and

possibly quite controversial way of praying. He suggested that we, like Jabez, pray for ourselves first. Many Christians would not agree. They may even consider it a sin to pray for yourself before praying for others. In fact, he suggested that we ask GOD for abundant blessings; not just a few. However, we all know that 'to whom much is given; much is expected.' The enlargement of one's territory means new and exciting opportunities. It also means new and more challenging missions.

I began starting every day with the prayer of Jabez. Without a doubt, it worked; God began blessing me with experiences that I never thought possible. In fact, there were so many experiences that I became a little overwhelmed. Even more overwhelming were the consequences of those blessings. Family members and people who had been close friends of mine for years began to change. I lost my father. Suddenly, I discovered that some of the people who I assumed would be my protectors were actually trying to hurt me. They could not be happy about my blessings and jealousy took over. I found myself having to set limits or sever long term ties with people. It was lonely and frightening. So I decided to stop praying Jabez's prayer because it was too overwhelming.

I continued to pray daily. I just did not pray the Jabez prayer. Things settled down and my territory continued to grow but at a much more manageable pace. A few years went by and I grew stronger and wiser.

God began to place different, more positive and encouraging people in my path. Suddenly I realized that most of the people that I spent my time with were actively interested in my success. I also noticed that my gift of discernment helped me to weed potentially toxic people out of my life.

Those realizations brought on a new realization. It was time for me to go back to praying the prayer of Jabez; this time with a renewed commitment. I made the commitment to make the Jabez prayer a part of my daily prayer ritual. No matter what happened, I would "stand" and keep praying. My borders began to enlarge in ways that

I had never considered. My thinking began to change and I found myself consulting GOD for everything. I also began doing the things that GOD told me to do. If he told me to visit a church I hadn't gone to before, I went. If he told me to call or write someone I was out of touch with, I did. Whatever I believed GOD was pushing me to do I did. The more I did that, the more I discovered new opportunities.

Of course, there were consequences. There were people who seemed to turn against me for no apparent reason. There were still people around me that I knew I could not trust. I found myself being tried, tested and stretched. Many days I found myself praying the prayer through tears of frustration, fear, and exhaustion but I kept praying. For a while, I was afraid that nothing I tried would ever work.

Eventually, I reached what I believed to be a tipping point in my blessings. One of my most passionate prayers was answered. That blessing released a great deal of pressure. It also allowed me to clear my head a little, accept the prayers that had not been answered and figure out my next move. Again my thinking changed and I began considering doing things that I had never even thought about before.

I still have my share of frustrations and GOD certainly has not answered all of my prayers. Also, I'm pretty sure that I have more tests and trials to face. As GOD continues to enlarge my territory, he will continue to stretch and test me. However, it is absolutely clear to me that the blessings that I will enjoy as a result of the prayer are worth every challenge that I will face to receive them.

关 系

Relationship

RELATIONSHIPS

When we hear the word relationship we most often think of romantic relationships. Don't forget that you have a relationship with everyone that you know.

"Know when to cut your loses."
      Sometimes we remain involved with people because they owe us money or we did something for them and we think that they should reciprocate. Or we remain on a job waiting to be appreciated. If you have made a reasonable attempt to get your needs met in a relationship or on a job and you still feel like you are losing out, move on. Chalk what you have already lost up to experience and take yourself out of a losing situation.

"When someone makes you choose between loving yourself and loving him or her, choose to love yourself."

"If you live for him, and he lives for him, then who lives for you?" **DeShera Rainey**

"All new relationships are magical for a while but magic is just a temporary illusion. Make sure that your relationships have the substance to outlast the magic." **T. Hurley Johnson**

"Boys want quantity, while men seek quality." **Jawanza Kunjufu**

"You don't have the time or energy to spend on someone else's frailties." **DeShera Rainey**

"Animals fight because they can't talk...Let's talk it over." **Linda A. Howard Curtis**

"The greatest thing that your mate can do for you is to be capable of taking care of him or her self both financially and emotionally."

It is perfectly all right for you to lean on each other from time to time. No one can be expected to be strong all the time. However, each of you should be able to take care of yourself.

"You never know how bound you are until you set yourself free."

When you are in a relationship that is not working it can be draining. You can become so used to being depleted that you don't even try to change things. Use the energy that you have left to free yourself. Once you have done that, you will be able to look back and see how oppressive the relationship was.

"If he doesn't know what to do with his heart, how will he know what to do with yours?"

"Learn to live with discomfort."

Making positive changes in your life can cause discomfort, especially when it involves telling someone how you feel or setting boundaries with someone who is close to you. It is important to understand that having someone angry or disappointed because you do what's best for you will make you uncomfortable but it is something that you can live with.

"Do not get married just for the wedding."

"Don't expect to get something from someone who only knows how to take."

"There is nothing wrong with marriage that sacrifice and compromise can't conquer."
Jawana Kunfuju

"When you feel that you have to test someone, they are very likely to fail." **Whitteney Guyton**

"If someone is paying you or teaching you something, they don't have to take your crap!"

"The best defense is a good offense. Remember that when someone tries to tell you that it is your fault when they mistreat you." **Juanita Hobson**

"Young people refer to falling in love as 'catching feelings.'"
When they put it that way it seems like love is the equivalent of "cooties" and it doesn't sound like much fun.

"Leaving a relationship in which you are undervalued is like dislocating a shoulder."
The first thing a doctor does with a dislocated shoulder is pull it into place. This hurts much worse but the shoulder begins to heal immediately. Soon the pain stops. If you don't pull the shoulder (leave the relationship) you never heal and the pain continues indefinitely.

"Holding on to resentment is like hitting yourself in the head every day and hoping the other person will feel it." **Lisa Smith**

"For a relationship to work, you must have the 3 C's. Commitment, Communication and Compromise." **Andrew Tate**

"No matter what the situation, there's never a reason to be less than decent!"
Mary Callais

"I met the man (or woman) of my dreams and then I woke up."

Two years ago, I bought a new car. I remember spending lots of time thinking about the make and model I wanted. I spent even more time deciding accessories and color. Determining what I absolutely had to have, what I liked but could live without and what I definitely did not want. Next I looked into what I could bring to the table. I asked myself: How much money do I have? What am I willing to pay to get what I want? Will I negotiate and compromise?

Once I had done my research, I went to Toyota. I told the salesperson, John Randle, exactly what I was looking for. He took me for a test drive in a car that was the correct make and model. I loved it. However it was missing the things that I had decided I couldn't live without. I smiled and politely explained that I wanted to buy my car from him and I was willing to wait if he could get me the one I wanted.

A week later, I got a call from John. The

car that I wanted was on the lot and ready for me to pick it up. I thanked him and rushed over to complete the best car buying experience of my life. As I was driving my beautiful new car off the lot, I had a sobering thought. I thought, if only I had put that much consideration into choosing my last boyfriend.

How do you go about choosing a mate? I'm often amazed at the answer I get to this question. Everything from "I don't know" to "I like the way he/she looks in tight jeans". Many of us chose a partner by default. We pick the person who likes us or needs us. We pick the one that looks the best or has the most or (my personal favorite) that one who happens to be around.

I wish I could give you one surefire formula that would work for everyone. Unfortunately, human beings tend to be unpredictable. I can however, give you a basic outline to follow. You can add your own 'twist' to it:

First, get to know yourself. In my opinion, after your relationship with GOD, the most important relationship you have is with you. It's important to know what you bring to the table. After all, how will you know what you want if you don't know who you are?

Second, think about the characteristics that you want your spouse to have. Make a list of the ones that are most important and learn to recognize them when you see them. Also, know what you don't want.

Third, consider how you will be able to work together. Understand that your partner should have strengths that you may not have and vice versa. Looking for someone who is just like you could have disadvantages.

Finally, don't forget that physical attraction is great but that alone will not sustain a healthy relationship.

忠告

js

Advice

SIMPLE ADVICE FOR A GOOD LIFE

These "one-liners" can be used to prevent all kinds of mistakes.

"You are stronger than you think."

"You are smarter than you think."

"You can take more than you think."

"You can do more than you think."

"Know your limit and don't reach it."
Bernard Orie

"When you know that you are in a hole STOP DIGGING!" **unknown**

"Life is change." **Judson Laipply**

"If you feel something, say it. You may not get the chance later on." **Dave Frederick**

"What comes from the heart reaches the heart." **unknown**

"Never get angry with someone for not giving you something you haven't asked for."

"If we don't learn from our mistakes there is no need to make them." **T. Hurley Johnson**

"Short cuts usually don't pay off in the long run."

"If you call someone and get voice mail, always leave a message and your phone number. Don't make them look it up."

"You don't have to know everything. You just have to know who to ask."

"You should not allow your own anger to harm you."
Most of the time you hurt yourself much more if you hold on to anger.

"You can survive whatever you are afraid of."

"There are colors that you love and colors that love you. You should decorate with the colors that you love and wear the colors that love you."

"Do not end conversations with I'll call you back unless that is what you plan to do. That's just plan rude."

"Nothing beats a failure but a try." **Olivia Byrd**

"You cannot do anything well if you are trying to do everything. Learn to set priorities!"

"Procrastination is a thief! It steals time, money and peace of mind." **Jewel Diamond Taylor**

"When GOD has delivered you from people, then you are really free to serve him."
Jean C. Bellamy

"Why be a big fish in a little pond when you can swim in the ocean."

"Pronounce your words right and spell them right so folks won't think you are ignorant."
Melva Threatt Walker

"The lessons you learn the hard way are the lessons you learn the best." **Rebecca Yasky**

"There is an unseen hand directing and guiding you." **Stephanie Credle**

"The best way to make a fear go away is to face it."

"Do leave home without it." **Carolyn Hines**
     Carolyn's mother believes that credit cards are tools of Satan.

"You cannot control the behavior of other people. You can only control your reaction."
     Accepting this gives you unlimited power.

"Count your blessings and not your bruises."
Jewel Diamond Taylor

"GOD Loves you and wants you whole."
Al Lewis, Herbal Farmacy
     What Al means is that GOD wants you to be healthy physically, mentally, emotionally and spiritually.

"Life is 10% what happens to you and 90% how you react to it." **Tia Norde**

"We are all facilitators of our highest potential."
Gail Glassmoyer

"You must serve from your saucer not your cup."
Dr. Katie Davis

Katie explained it to me this way. My cup is my primary source of energy. She said that I must make sure that my cup is full to the point of overflow into my saucer. I serve others from my saucer (energy overflow) so I don't deplete my cup (primary energy source).

"Never call a guest in your home a visitor."
Valerie Snellings

A visitor normally just stops by and may be unexpected, while a guest is welcomed and much more treasured. Remember to treat a guest like a guest and a visitor like a visitor.

"Pain is GOD's reset button. It allows us to start over again stronger and wiser."
Jewel Diamond Taylor

"Character is not developed in hard times; character is revealed in hard times."
Jean C. Bellamy

"Don't let it beat, you beat it!" **James Wimbley**

"When we are at our lowest lows we find our greatest strengths."

"Never let anyone beat you at being nice!"
Rose M. Howard

"When voting or dating, look for the best one, not the perfect one."

"Worry is misuse of the imagination."
Michelle Pippin, Women Who Wow

"Today is tomorrow!"
Lisa Jacques, Sounds Yummy Pet Bakery
Don't put it off. Get on with it!

"It's a small thing to a giant!" **Courtney Stewart**
This was her father's way of telling her not to sweat the small stuff.

"Paying too much attention to problems will surely block your blessings."
Melva Threatt Walker

"If you tell the truth, you don't have to remember anything." **unknown Internet source**
Lying about something means you have to remember what lie you told and to whom. The truth is much easier to remember.

"If it is to be, it's up to me." **Latoya Corbin**

"Think before you speak...think twice before you act!" **Linda A. Howard Curtis**

"Generally speaking, you aren't learning much when your lips are moving."
unknown Internet source

"The door to success is labeled 'push.'"
Jewel Diamond Taylor

"There are many things in life that will catch your eye, but only a few that will catch your heart...pursue those!"
The Center for Metabolic Health

"Wash your hands and say your prayers. God and germs are invisible but they are everywhere."
Judith Orloff, MD.

"Everything has a home. Keep everything in its home and it won't ever get lost!"
Rose M. Howard

"Keep yourself open to positive energy."
Rosalind Tatum

"Like it or not,
you are a role model."

Human beings are social animals. It is
natural for us to develop relationships.
Sometimes these relationships are with
people you don't even know. Early in my
career, I realized that my personal life
was no longer entirely personal. I was in
my mid twenties and just a few years out
of grad school when I got a job as a
Career Counselor at an agency for
adolescents in New York City called The
Door, a holistic alternative agency,
worked with as many as 300 young
people a day aged 12 to 21.

My wake up call came when I was doing
an intake interview with a client who
was 17 years old. I asked what he liked
to do in his spare time and he said that
he liked going to clubs. He then
continued to name clubs, several of
which I also frequented. I remember
thinking, do I want to go out and have
this kid counting how many drinks I've
had and asking me to dance to slow
music? Or even worse what if I had
been at the club flirting with him and let
him buy me a drink. He was tall and
quite handsome. I would never have

known he was only 17 if he had not told me.

The thought made me realize that I no longer had the luxury of completely leaving work at the end of the day. No matter where I went or what I was doing, there would be a possibility that someone who knew me would be there. The thought also made me stop going to those clubs.

That is when I knew that, like it or not, good or bad, I was a role model. I no longer had a choice. That, relatively speaking, was the bad news. The good news was that I always had a choice about how I conducted myself. I decided that, if people would be taking their cues from my behavior, than I would just have to behave myself.

Please don't misunderstand me. I am just as imperfectly human as anyone else. I make mistakes and bad choices, get angry, laugh, cry, and 'bump my head' just like anyone else. However the thought that someone is watching and basing their behavior on mine is never far from my mind. That thought has certainly influenced my choices.

No matter who you are, what your job title is or how old you are there is always someone who could be basing their choices and behaviors on yours. It might be a son, daughter, sibling or neighbor. It might also be someone you don't know is watching.

The real question is this: Do you want the people who follow your lead to be poised and accomplished professionals, parents and mentors? Or do you want them to be criminals, victims, liars or losers? The choice is yours.

智慧

js

Wisdom

WORDS OF WISDOM FROM THE SCHOOL OF HARD KNOCKS

These sayings are the reason that "if I knew then what I know now" is a cliché.

"Your time and my time ain't GOD's time."
John Williams

"Never make someone a priority in your life if they treat you like an option." **Valerie Snellings**

"Take your emotions [i.e. fear, embarrassment, sadness] with you into new situations. Don't wait for them to go away, they probably will not."
The best way to overcome these potentially paralyzing emotions is to face them.

"Don't miss that concert, restaurant, movie, etc., because you don't have a date. Go with a friend if you can or take yourself."

"Courage is when you are scared to death but you do it anyway."

"You can't fail if you don't give up."

"PAY ATTENTION!!! It is amazing what you will miss if you don't."

"It is not a friendship, if it has not been tested."
T. Hurley Johnson

"At least once a week, you will be faced with a situation that gives you a chance to throw up your hands and say, 'I quit.'"
Before you do that, ask yourself what will or will not happen if you do.

"Marijuana is not the most dangerous drug but it is the sneakiest."

Marijuana affects you just as much when you are not high. Your motivation and short term memory continue to be affected after you smoke. You could find yourself ten years later in the same place you were ten years before. What is really scary is that you may not know why this is a problem.

"Cocaine will come into your life and kick you out."

You will become someone even you don't recognize.

"Surefire formula for good grades: go to class, pay attention, do your homework and study for your exams."

"The magnitude of your problems should be measured by the actual effect that they have on your life."

"The most devastating drug is the one you like the best." **Linda Hancock**

"If someone tells you that they want to kill themselves, tell somebody."

You'd rather them be alive and pissed off at you then dead because you kept their secret.

"Credit makes enemies. I wanna be friends."
Linda A. Howard Curtis

"Tough times don't last, but tough people do!"
Pastor Jerome Anthony Barber, Sixth Mount Zion Baptist Temple

"It is good to have an email address that never changes."
That way, friends whom you have not seen in years can still get in touch with you.

"A pity party is selfish and drains my energy and faith." **Jewel Diamond Taylor**

"Keep in touch with people who know your work."
A good network is worth its weight in gold.

"A person does not have to hit you to abuse you."
There are many forms of abuse that don't involve hitting. If you feel abused, most likely you've been abused.

"Beware of confusing love and lust."
Quite often a person who is very good at sex will be incredibly bad at love.

"The difference between a star and a superstar is motivation and perseverance."
Jewel Diamond Taylor

"Life is like a minefield."
You are more likely to know where the explosives are if you follow someone who has already been through the field.

"The one thing that no one can take from you is your education." **Cleon Disnew, Jr.**

"Never allow anyone to make you apologize for being who you are."
Please do not misunderstand this one. It does not mean that you can use or mistreat people and use "that's just who I am" as an excuse.

"Give yourself permission to enjoy what is enjoyable."
When you are feeling good or having a good time, don't diminish it by worrying that something will go wrong. Just enjoy it!

"The proper response to a compliment is a smile and a thank you."
Don't respond to a compliment by putting yourself down. It's insulting to you and the person who gave you the compliment.

"Procrastination is overwhelming."
Putting things off creates stress. The longer you put something off, the more stressful it becomes.

"Use every tool you have."
When you are trying to reach a goal or accomplish something, find every tool that will help. Make use of everything that is available.

"It **is** possible for confidence and humility to coexist."
These traits are not opposites. It is feasible and beneficial to be both. We are given certain gifts and talents by GOD. As a result we should be confident of our abilities. For the same reason we should also be humble. It is GOD working through us that makes us talented and gifted.

"Grown is not a number."
Simply being 21 doesn't make you grown. Grown means stepping up, taking responsibility for your actions and accepting the consequences of your choices. When you are able to do that, you are grown.

"Sometimes better is the best that you are going to get."
Don't wait for the perfect conditions. They probably won't come.

"Aging puts wrinkles on the body. Quitting puts wrinkles on the soul." **Jewel Diamond Taylor**

"People see you whether you think they are looking or not." **Duane Thompson**

"The main thing is to keep the main thing the main thing!" **Jewel Diamond Taylor**

When you have a purpose there will always be opportunities to do things that move you off of your path. Some of them will sound really good and be very tempting. Don't forget your purpose!

"If you hang around with 3 broke people (*potheads, scholars, etc.*), you will be the fourth." **Carolyn Hines**

"You are not a woman until you: get a job, get out on your own, get your `self a husband." **Roslyn Durham**

Roslyn said that this momma saying changed at each stage of her life. When she accomplished one her mother would come up with a new one

"In order to keep your integrity, do not agree to anything you do not agree with."

In other words, don't do anything that you think is wrong or that makes you uncomfortable just because someone else wants you to.

"The way you look and dress announces how you feel about yourself and you'll be treated accordingly." **Sandra Dumont, The Image Architect**

"If you see someone without a smile, give them one of yours." **Barbara Smith**

"If you are interested, you will do what's convenient. If you are committed, you will do what ever it takes!" **Lisa Smith**

"Thought creates emotion. Emotion creates action. Action creates results."
Michelle Pippin, Women Who Wow

"Sometimes you just have to feel what you feel."
There are times when holding your feelings in or hiding them is a lot more damaging to you than letting them out. You'd be surprised to see how much allowing yourself to feel helps you to heal.

"Always remember these two things and you will be successful. No one is better than you and no one is worse than you."
Harold (Barney) Wilson

"People will forget what you said, people will forget what you did, but people will never forget how you made them feel." **unknown**

"Intelligent people do not always make intelligent choices but they are still intelligent people."
Don't judge your intellect or that of others by the choices that are made. None of us gets it right all the time.

"Problems are the platforms for your promotion." **Pastor Jerome Anthony Barber, Sixth Mount Zion Baptist Temple**

"It isn't about waiting for the storm to pass; it is about learning to dance in the rain."
Michelle Pippin, Women Who Wow

"Even if you are on the right track, you will get run over if you just sit there." **Shari Wilson**

"Don't be afraid of enduring pain to reach your promise. Surgery hurts after it's done, but you are better off once you are healed." **Jon-Al Sawyer**

"We all do the best we can at the time with what we have...spiritually, physically, mentally, emotionally and financially!" **Mary Callais**

"Surround yourself with people who are not afraid to introduce you to yourself."

I was applying for a new job. I was admittedly a little concerned about my qualifications because I'm not yet finished with my Doctorate. When I saw the online advertisement, the first person I called was Dr. Katie Davis, my mentor and "Other Mother." I had three requests. I wanted to know if she would: read my letter of application, write a recommendation letter for me, and meet me for lunch a few days later. She agreed to all of my requests.

At lunch, later that week, she greeted me with the kind of genuine affection that lets you know that you are loved; the kind of love that you just bask in. After we were shown to our table, we chatted briefly with the waitress. We placed our orders and settled in to "catch up" with each other's busy lives.

The waitress brought our plates and drinks. Once the food was blessed we each picked up our forks. As I began to eat, Katie pulled a folder out of her purse and pushed it over to me. "You did say a letter of application right?" she asked. "Yes, I did." I replied. "In that case, I want you to rewrite this. This is a cover letter not a letter of application."

My response was to put my fork down and grab a pen and paper. "Lori, there are so many wonderful things about you that are not in this letter. You must sell yourself to these people." I said "Yes Ma'am." She talked while I scribbled furiously. Being the consummate educator that she is, she did not offer me one word of dictation; she gave me themes. "Your first paragraph should address this, your next that" and so on. When she finished, it did not have a new letter, I had an outline for a new letter.

I was not one bit discouraged by her criticism. I went home, rewrote the letter and sent it to her. "This letter is blessed" was her response. Then she wrote me a letter of recommendation that was so beautiful that I put it in a frame.

On the mat around the letter, I had the saying that was inspired by this incident written in calligraphy. A few weeks later,

I had the pleasure of taking Katie to lunch, showing her the framed letter and sharing this story with her. That letter will hang in the office of my next job and every job I get after that.

幽默

is

Humor

FROM THE
CHUCKLE FACTORY

*These sayings may not be
"politically correct" but they may
make you laugh.*

"I don't wish you bad luck but I hope good luck catches you on the corner and beats the hell out of you." **James "Poppa" Hobson**

"You have two choices. You can live in my house and do what I say or you can do what I say and live in my house." **Constance Jermin**

"I had to be inspected to be accepted."
Cyril Jermin
   This refers to asking for his wife's hand in marriage.

"Life isn't always the party we hope for but while you are here, you might as well dance."
Judson Laipply

"Eventually you will need a college degree to wash dishes." **Amber Roach**

"If you want to make GOD laugh, tell him YOUR plans." **unknown**

"Learn to say, 'So what' it will set you free."

"I'm allergic to exercise."
Eve Niles, www.youravon.com/evelynianiles

"If you are around more than ten people, you are bound to encounter at least one jerk."

"He who beds, weds." **Jimmy Poppa Hobson**

"When you are getting a free ride, don't try to drive. Just shut up and enjoy the ride."

"Do a mean telephone. It may take several calls to get what you need but if you really need it, be patient and make the calls."

"Don't start me to lying."
I think that there is somebody in every family who says this.

"I hate mean people."
Many of the emotional scars that people carry around have come from people who were mean.

"Come home at a reasonable hour. The only thing open late at night and in the wee hours is somebody's legs and they will not be yours!"
Carolyn Hines
Please understand that this saying is not meant to be vulgar. It is simply a very colorful way of telling a young woman what not to do.

"If you don't really want to know, don't ask."

"I can RSVP any argument. Sorry I can't come."
Jewel Diamond Taylor

"I was on a see-food diet. If I see food, I eat it!"
Eve Niles, www.youravon.com/evelynianiles

"When I said please I was not asking you, I was telling you politely."

"Don't place yourself in a sexual situation that causes your mind and body to go to war. Your body will win and mess it and your mind up."

"I don't mind giving you my money if you give me my money's worth."

"The more you have to do, the less you'll want to do later."
Busy people don't have time for procrastination.

"Just because somebody asks what you think doesn't mean they have to do what you say."

"When trying to lose weight, there's one fast rule. IF IT TASTES GOOD, SPIT IT OUT!"

"I love you enough to risk your wrath."
The people who love you the most are the one's who will risk angering you by telling the truth.

"Good sex makes the obvious hard to see."
Jocyllin "Nana" Catrez *(age 100 plus)*

"You can't apply logic to stupidity. It won't work."

"In some neighborhoods common sense doesn't live on the whole block." **Barbara Bazemore**

"If I can't teach you I'll learn you." **Gregory Fox**

"This is a character building exercise."
Jennifer Hooks
This is what her father would tell her when she was being punished for something she did wrong.

"Misery loves company but it can't get none of mine." **Wise Warren**

"The foreplay for the sex you want tomorrow night should have started yesterday." **Olivia Byrd**
Gentlemen if you don't understand this one, you need to have a long talk with your wife.

"If it's wet and it's not yours, DON'T TOUCH IT!" **Linda Hancock**
Linda is a nurse practitioner who treats many STD's.

"My mother didn't raise any stupid children."
Juanita Hobson

"Mom made all of the decisions but if she made the wrong one Dad would let her know."
Rusty Richards

"No is a complete sentence. Not the beginning of a negotiation." **Olivia Byrd**

"Life requires effort!"

"Never pass up the offer of a breath mint. It's probably a hint!" **Lisa Smith**

"When the rum done, the fun done!"
Jimmy Poppa Hobson

"There's never time to do a thing right but there's always time to do a thing over." **Rusty Richards**
It is better to get it right the first time.

"One day you are going to open your mouth and I'm going to come out."
I tell my Goddaughters that one all the time.

"His/her mouth ain't no prayer book."
Olivia Byrd
Olivia was explaining that anyone can lie. You must examine what people say before you assume they are telling the truth.

"Stop crying before I give you something to cry about." **Juanita Hobson**
Unfortunately my mother always said this after she had given me something to cry about.

"You can't make chicken salad out of chicken @#*! No matter what you do to it."
Lawrence Dotolo

"I love sex. I ain't lying but none of your sex is worth me dying." **Wise Warren**

"A.D.G.O. Another Darned Growth Opportunity!" **Linda Hancock**
That's when you make some awful mistake that forces you to grow.

"It is so good to be seen and not viewed."
Jewel Diamond Taylor

"I speak busy fluently."
This one came to me when I was trying to go on a date and both of us had to take out our PDA's to find a time when we would be available.

"You are beautiful but you are not here to decorate my house."
You need to go to school or go to work or both. You can't just sit around the house. My daughter can tell you about this one.

"You eat here, you sleep here, you work here."
Leona LaPerriere

"God gave you two pockets baby, use them!"
Kyshsia Wynn
Kyshia's grandmother used this saying to tell her about putting valuables in the "bra bank".

"The only thing constant is change and here we go again!" **Denise Cherry**

"I know I look like a size 16 but I'm really a size 16 covering a size 10 so she doesn't get scratched." **Jewel Diamond Taylor**

"Momma said there'd be days like this but she never said they'd come so often."
Janice B. Holland

"If at first you don't succeed, skydiving is probably not for you."
unknown Internet source

"You've got to crawl before you walk but you shouldn't have to wear out your kneecaps."
Wise Warren

"Oh, Miss Grand Marnier. Drink her too fast and she will knock you out of your rocking chair!"
Theresa DeWitt

"If you do that, your tail is going to drag on the ground." **Judy Bander**
This meant that whatever you are about to do will be the beginning of your financial and/or social downfall and humiliation.

"Karma is crazy! Just when you think she is gone, she will sneak up behind you."
Marvin DeWitt, Jr.

"Never miss a good chance to shut up!"
unknown Internet source

"Quit whining and get to stepping! Whiners sound and look plain stupid!"
Melva Threatt Walker

"If you lend someone $20 and never see that person again; it was probably a wise investment."
unknown Internet source

"If you have drama with everyone around you, remember **you** are the common denominator."
Jean Bellamy

"Thank GOD I don't look like what I've been through!" **Jewel Diamond Taylor**

"From the top of your neck to the bottom of your nose is all yours but, every two weeks the top of your head belongs to the barbershop!"
Myron Bennett James

"Just 'cause you don't see the devil don't mean he ain't there!" **Renee Edwards**

"The nicest thing about not planning is that failure comes as a complete surprise and is not proceeded by a period of worry and depression."
Kathy Kormen Frey, The Hot Momma Project

"Act your age, not your shoe size." **Marisa Harris**

"You don't hate me because I think I'm all that, you hate me because you think I'm all that."

What does success look like to you? How do you define it? Is it writing a book, building a business or making a certain amount of money? Clearly success looks different to different people. Equally clear is that success looks quite different from the inside than it looks from the outside. Those of us who are working to build something for ourselves and our children can relate to the long hours, setbacks and disappointments. We know what it took to get that house, that car, those clothes, etc.

When you pursue your dreams you may expect to encounter certain obstacles. Things like lack of financing, time or support. When you are a member of a minority group (this includes females), you expect to meet people who don't believe in you because of who or what you are.

There is one thing that goes with the territory that could easily blindside you.

That thing is haters. A hater is a person who cannot handle your success. He or she is bothered by the fact that you have been blessed. A hater is someone who wants what you have but doesn't want to or can't do what is necessary to get it. Unfortunately they are quite often the people who are closest to you.

One of the things that I learned about myself years ago was that I have a 'light' that people find attractive. Most of the time people are attracted to my light and they want to talk to me, be in my presence, ask me questions, etc. It's great and it makes me a good friend, counselor, speaker and trainer.

However there are a small percentage of people who are also attracted to my light but want to put it out. When I realized this, I tried (to no avail) to hide my light so people wouldn't try to hurt me. It didn't take long to figure out that it is impossible to hide your light, especially from those who are most intimidated by it.

In the message *Our Greatest Fear*, Marianne Williamson says in part, "Our greatest fear is not that we are inadequate, but that we are powerful beyond measure. It is our light, not our darkness that frightens us. There is nothing enlightened about shrinking so that other people won't feel insecure around you." My interpretation of Marianne's comments is that you should be who you really are always. Don't attempt to hide your light and don't let haters put it out.

A friend and mentor once told me that the difference between a star and a superstar is motivation and perseverance. When people hate on you it means that you are doing something right. The next time you encounter a hater tell them, you don't hate me because I think I'm all that, you hate me because you think I'm all that. Look them in the eye and tell them to **BRING IT**!

爱自己

js

Love Yourself

TO KNOW YOURSELF IS TO LOVE YOURSELF

Besides your relationship with GOD, the most important relationship that you have is with yourself.

"I will be the president of your fan club until you can take over."

"Every once in a while, treat yourself to something that looks, feels, sounds, tastes or smells good."

"If you hurt my baby, I'll have to kill you."
My Goddaughters hear this one all the time. It means it's not okay with me for anybody to hurt them. Not even them. If they do something to hurt themselves, watch out!

"Learn to enjoy your own company and others will enjoy you too."

"Be your own best friend or biggest fan."

"Always love yourself from within. GOD loves you and expects you to do the same."

"The more you love yourself, the easier you are to love."
When you don't love yourself you tend to be needy and neurotic and it takes too much energy to love you.

"As you become more aware of your worth, you become less tolerant of those who are not."

"Oh the familiar comfort of my discomfort."
Sometimes people stay in terrible situations simply because they are used to them.

"Be an asset, not a trophy."
An asset is something valuable that appreciates over time. A trophy is something that sits on a shelf looking pretty and collecting dust.

"It is very unhealthy to put yourself last all of the time."

"Wear conversation pieces."
If you want to be noticed when you are out, wear something that makes you stand out. For example, a well fitting suit in an unusual color or style or a signature tie or necklace. People will remember you or talk to you because of what you are wearing.

"You don't wear your clothes inside out. Nobody knows what size they are unless you tell them."
Juanita Hobson

"Whether it is a 2 or 52. Always buy your size!"
Nothing is less flattering than wearing something that is too big if you are petite or too small if you are plus sized.

"You don't have time to be the object of someone else's insecurities."

"There is always a cost. Nothing is free."
It may cost you time, energy, sleep or friends.
The real question is; is it worth it?

"Walk with a high head and a virtuous butt."
Carolyn Hines

"Learn what your God given gifts and talents are and USE THEM!"
You can find out what they are by visiting www.gifttest.org and taking the free survey.

"Never be ashamed to tell your age. You either get old or you die young." **Louise Brown**

"If you are the most intelligent person in the room, then you are in the wrong room."

"Consider it a compliment when people talk bad about you. You must be mighty important if all they can find to talk about is you."
Juanita Hobson

"The only limitations in your life are those dictated by your own thinking." **Lisa Smith**

"Just because they make it in your size doesn't mean you should wear it."

"You were born GOD's original, try not to become someone's copy." **Marion Wright Edelman, Children's Defense Fund**

"Sexy is a state of mind."

I have to begin this story with a disclaimer. What is really sexy is a matter of opinion. With that said, I welcome the opportunity to give you mine. Take it from someone who has been on the planet for more years than she cares to remember, sexy is a state of mind.

Showing lots of skin and lots of cleavage will certainly get a man's attention. However, a confident strut coupled with a subtle hip sway while covered from head to toe will get his attention and his respect. (Attention and respect is a great combination.) The former may prompt him to invite you in (for example into his bed, a hotel or a back seat). The latter will encourage him to invite you out (in public) without assuming he can invite you in.

The latter will also attract a different type of man; one who you can actually talk to. Most women have experienced trying to have a conversation with a man who is leering at you. Frankly, I'd rather converse with a man who is looking me in the eye than one who is staring below my neck or my navel.

In business, being too overtly sexy can be a real slippery slope. If you have the sexiness that comes with confidence and self love, it can work in your favor. When a man finds you attractive, he may be more interested in doing business with you. However, if your sexiness takes the form of wearing your blouses down low and your skirts up high he may want to do more than business.

If, for example, your legs are your best feature and you want to show them off then of course go for it. Just be very careful about how you conduct yourself. You don't want a man to think that your body is part of your business contract and you would be amazed at how often that happens. Ladies, I know it's not fair and it's not right but it is the world we live in.

If someone were to ask me to sum up what is sexy to me in one word, that word would be confidence. A man who knows who he is and is comfortable with who I am will get my attention every time, regardless of how he looks. On the other hand, I have a hard time taking a man seriously when he comes at me crotch first. I don't find bragging about what you can or will do in bed sexy. Especially when it comes from a man I hardly know.

Have you ever met someone who you don't find physically attractive but there is something about them that is still inexplicably sexy? Sexy is more about how you feel about yourself then how you look, whether you are male or female. There are large people, small people, light people, dark people , etc., who love and value themselves. That can make them very sexy.

When trying to decide if you want your sex appeal to be overtly over the top or subtlety sensuous, you should ask yourself two questions then carry yourself accordingly:

(1) What are you looking for? A man you can look up **to** in a meaningful relationship or a man you can look up **at** on a "one night stand?"

(2) Do you want to be considered sexy because you are showing as much of your body as possible or because you are fantastic and you know it?

Mary J. Blige has a song in which she sings "I'm so sexy, remain a mystery 'cause everybody always wants what they can't see and what they can't have and what they can't grab and what they can't buy and baby that's me!" I'm with Mary J.

女人

js

Woman

WOMAN TO WOMAN

When I'm talking to a young woman who is down on herself, I often say "It's all right baby. You just bumped your head that's all. You will be okay." Maybe some of these sayings will prevent other young women from bumping their heads.

"A man loving you won't necessarily stop him from cheating on you, beating on you, using or abusing you."

"You are more likely to get a man to do something for you if say please help me instead of you better do it."

"Sometimes the fat girl wins."
Don't think that your weight will keep you in or out of the running. There is a reason that we come in all shapes and sizes.

"I love men. They look good, smell good and lie good." **Carole DeRouen**

"If you can't find mister right, look in your mirror."
Always take the best care of yourself that you possibly can.

"Always treat yourself better than any man treats you."

"Pay yourself first." **Olivia Byrd**
Even if it's just a tube of lipstick or a pair of stockings, you should buy something just for you on a regular basis.

"What is easy doesn't make a woman happy."
Martine Hutton

"A wise woman builds her house; A foolish woman tears it down with her own hands. Proverbs 14:1" **Christine Nelson**

"In the long run, the stress of not having a man in your life is much less than the stress of having the wrong man in you life. *DO NOT SETTLE!*"

"If you are out with your man and his clothes are newer and/or better than yours, there is something very wrong with that picture."

"Needy is scary."
Being a "damsel in distress" may get the man but it won't necessarily keep him. Constantly needing to be rescued will eventually turn him off. If you want to scare a man away or change his attitude toward you, act needy all the time.

"For women, the three biggest challenges are: Your money, Your tummy and Your honey." **Jewel Diamond Taylor**

"You must look at the prize to know if you have lost. "
If a man who makes you miserable leaves you for another woman, YOU WIN!

"Men marry hoping a woman will not change and women marry hoping a man will change." **Jewel Diamond Taylor**

"The greatest player move is to tell the truth."
It sounds something like this. I love my girlfriend or wife but you are so hard to resist.(This is not man bashing, it is player bashing)

"If GOD made anything more beautiful than a good man, he kept it for himself and that is alright with me."

"Girl you are sitting on a million dollars!"
Kaille Viney
This saying is a message to young women about valuing their bodies and waiting until the time is right to have sex.

"My husband never forgot our anniversary or my birthday because I didn't let him."
Juanita Hobson
Mom would remind him of these dates and tell him exactly what he was going to buy her. Dad was happy because he didn't have to guess what she wanted or get into trouble because he forgot. It was a "win-win" situation.

"It takes one to get over one."
(Interview with Kelly Buffaloe)

This is probably the only Momma Saying in the book that is not recommended by the contributor or the author. It and the story behind it are included as an example of what not to do. Kelly has told me empathically that she will not pass this one on to her daughter. After hearing her story and the reason for her decision, I don't think that I would pass it on to my daughter either.

When Kelly was a teenager, she was hurt after breaking up with her boyfriend. Her mother offered her advice that she had gotten from her own mother. She said, "It takes one to get over one." Meaning that, to get over a breakup, you need to find somebody new. Kelly took this advice to heart and decided that she would always have a "reserve boyfriend." The "reserve boyfriend" wasn't as important to her as the primary one. He would just be around as backup in case things didn't work out with the primary beau. Kelly's reserve boyfriend method stuck with her until she went to college.

When Kelly went to college, she had a

serious relationship with one of the star basketball players. He was not drafted right out of school and had to go through the process of trying out. This often kept him away from her and, since it was during the pre cell phone days, out of touch. Kelly, feeling slighted, decided that she would bring in the "second string." She started dating the reserve boyfriend. He did not have as much going for him as the primary but, after all, it takes one to get over one.

When her basketball star came back in to town and called, her response was "sorry but I've moved on." That young man went on to play on more than one NBA team. Eventually, he became a coach and went on to win the much-revered title of NBA Coach of the Year. To make things worse, on the night that he and Kelly broke up, he met the woman that he is married to now.

Kelly admitted that, for a while, she felt as if she made a terrible mistake and was unable to follow the career of her ex. Her friends teased her about missing out on "living in the big house." She and I laughed together at the thought that we don't know if she would have been happier, but she sure would have been richer!

That experience taught Kelly that the reserve method boyfriend might not be such a good idea after all. Today, Kelly is fine with the way her life has turned out. She gave up the habit of having a reserve boyfriend and was happily married for a number of years until her husband passed away. She is involved in a strong, healthy relationship that is headed toward marriage. Looking back with the 20-20 hindsight that we all develop with age, she left me with the following observation. "Thinking back, I wondered why my grandmother would say that. She only had one husband." Kelly's mother, the person who offered her this "Momma Saying," has been divorced twice, widowed once, and is currently involved again. "It seems that my mother really took it to heart" Kelly said with a smile.

At the end of the interview Kelly told me that she would never pass this saying on to her child. Instead she would tell her daughter to work on healing herself after a breakup. Once she has begun her healing process, then she can think about moving into a new relationship. It is the same advice that I have passed on to my daughter and hundreds of my clients.

家庭

js

Family

PARENTING

Parenting would be easy if it weren't for the kids.

"You could have come home
to a different mother."

When I told Linda that I was planning to add a parenting chapter to the book, she offered me the following true story that was told to her by a friend.

This woman had a teenage son. He was a good boy but he was also a typical teenager. They had a pretty good relationship and there were clear rules and expectations for everyone in the house. One of those rules was that her son had a clearly established curfew.

One night, this mother realized that it was past curfew time and her son was not at home yet. He also had not called. Any parent can tell you about the feelings that this type of experience can bring out. At first, you may be angry because he knows the rules and he has broken one of them. Then your mind begins to create all kinds of terrible possibilities. What if he was in an accident? Maybe he's lying in a ditch or in a hospital, or jail, or even worse, what if he's dead? At that point, anger yields to terror and there is no chance of getting back to sleep.

Unable to return to sleep, this mother goes into the living room to wait up for her son. Eventually, she hears his key in the door. Relief floods through her; followed by fury. When he walks in, she lets him have it. "Where have you been? You should have been home by curfew! Don't you know you scared me to death? What is wrong with you anyway?

Her son decides that he doesn't want to deal with her and starts up the stairs to bed. "Get back here" she yells. "I'm not finished with you. How dare you walk away from me?" Tired and now frustrated, her son turns to her and yells back. "You know what? I could have been out using drugs or drinking and driving. I could have been having unprotected sex or breaking the law. I wasn't doing anything wrong. I was just hanging out with my friends!"

His mother, however, was not going to be outdone or dismissed by her son. She retorted, "Yes and you could have come home to a mother who didn't care enough to give you a curfew. You could have come home to a mother who was using drugs and drinking. You could have come home to a cold house with an empty refrigerator. You didn't. You came home to a parent who cares enough to be worried and angry with you. Now get back down here so we can discuss this!"

That was as much of the story as I got.

Who knows who won that particular battle? The point is, as parents, there are times when we must stand up to the wrath of our children. While it is important that we listen to them and learn from them, there will inevitably be times when we know best.

Unfortunately it will probably take years for our children to realize that. If we are lucky, they admit it to us. If not, we just have to observe the way they conduct themselves to figure it out.

Linda Hancock

"Babies are wonderful. They are so cute and cuddly. Then they grow up and turn into people!" **Carole DeRouen**

"Rule # 1—Have fun! And 'fun' means 'fun for everyone.'" **Laurie Gray**

"We raise our children to be progressively independent of us and dependent on God." **Janet Thompson, author of Praying for Your Prodigal Daughter: Hope, Help & Encouragement for Hurting Parents**

"Tutto passa. The literal translation is everything passes." **Carol Casey**

"Sometimes you have to be like a state trooper with your kids." **Linda Hancock**
Linda got this one from a colleague. He said that when a State Trooper pulls you over, he/she doesn't yell at you. He/she simply asks if you know why you have been stopped. If you say no, you are told what you did wrong. Then they go on to give you a ticket or a warning or they arrest you. They do all of that without an excess of emotion. To them it is very clear. This is the law. You broke the law. These are the consequences; the end. When you have set rules to preserve the safety and sanity of your family and they are broken, you have to issue consequences. It is not easy but it is absolutely necessary.

"Because I said so." **Shari Wilson**

"Keep your spiritual light burning!"
Angela Sage Larsen

"I hope that someday you have a house full of children that act just like you." **unknown**
I call this one the mother's curse.

"God's favor surrounds us (our family) as shield and we have favor with everyone that we deal with today." **Djuana Daniel**

"Your kids don't alway want your advice. Sometimes you have to just listen!"
Paige French

"You always have options." **Dwight Bain**

"Pray, laugh, give lots of hugs and find a faith community for your family." **Lana Noone, www.vietnambabylift.org**

"If you are not living a virtuous life, your home and family will be in chaos." **Christine Nelson**

"I don't care what your counselor at school says about your future God has the last word."
Ann Beete-Graham

"Our family saying is 'IBIM' – I Believe In ME/ Miracles." **Karen Froneck, mother of 5**

"Kids grow up to be as dumb as they think their parents are." **Latoya Corbin**

"The angel of the LORD encamps all around our children and delivers them from perilous situations. We bless our children that they may be powerful in the land, and fulfill their divine destiny. We have no greater joy than this: to hear that our children are living their lives in the truth." Psalm 34:7 (Amplified Bible)
Djuana Daniel

"When children are little, the problems are small. When children get big, the problems get big."
Dr. Marlene Caroselli

"You live and you learn." **Marisa Harris**

"God knows. You don't!" *(I have two daughters, ages 9 and 5. My 9 year old sometimes wants to be "mommy" and thinks she knows everything. One day she said: "I want to be like you because you know everything." Of course, I laughed because this is farthest from the truth! I told her that the only one that knows everything is God. I said when you think you know everything and have to be right all the time, just remember: "God knows, you don't.")*
Stacey M. Hayes

"My parents always say 'Give me my flowers while I'm alive'." **Derrick Hayes**

"Sometimes mother knows best."
Kristi De Rouen-Jamison
Kristi said that, for years she did her best to prove her mother wrong; most of the time she was unsuccessful. Finally, when she was in her mid-twenties, it occurred to her that her mother loved her more than anything else. She realized that her mother would not knowingly tell her anything wrong.

"You don't get to pick the cross in life that you may have to carry, but you can pick how you will carry it." **Dwight Bain**

"Your choices are your choices."

Learning to say that to your children and mean it can be the key to sanity for most parents. My own parenting experience, working with parents, and my experience facilitating parenting groups have taught me that.

We have all heard about "the terrible twos" where your child discovers the word NO and turns it on you. Or the "tweens" where they suddenly discover the opposite sex and become a little "strange." Then there are of course those teenaged years where you become convinced that someone came along, took your child away and left this "evil twin" in his or her place.

There could be a considerable amount of debate about which of those stages is worse. That all depends on who you ask and what stage of development their child is in. I won't venture an opinion about which stage is worse but I will say that I believe that parents are most helpless at the end of those teen years and the beginning of young adulthood. That is when your ability to "pull rank" as a parent is severely limited.

You must allow your children to make their own choices and their own mistakes. You can prepare them to the best of your ability. Make sure they have a working knowledge of what is right and wrong, advise them, warn them, and pray for them. Then you have to step back and allow them to sink or swim.

The following is the analogy that I use to explain it: One of the most difficult experiences in the world is having to watch your beloved child running full speed toward a brick wall. You take a look at that formidable wall and say to your child "baby there's a wall over there, you are headed straight for it and you are going to hit it. Your baby looks over at you and, with all the wisdom of his or her time on the planet, and says "Yes mom/dad I know there is a wall but, after all, this is me and when I get there that wall is going to move!!"

At that point, your child has made a choice, whether you agree or not. The best thing you can do is be there to kiss the "boo-boo" and help them dry their tears. There are simply some mistakes your children are going to make no matter what you do or say. Failing to intervene will be painful at first but you will be pleasantly surprised at how quickly you can get over it. The greatest lesson that any human being can learn, is that there are consequences attached to every choice. To be good at it you have to bump your head a few times.

When I was about 25 years old I experienced an epiphany that has stuck with me. It is something that I have shared with whoever would listen to me ever since. I realized that I was not grown when I was 18; nor was I grown when I was 21. However, if anyone had dared to suggest such an outrageous thing to me at those ages, I would have quite self-righteously had then flogged. It wasn't until I actually reached maturity that I discovered how immature I had been up to that point.

During those "quasi-grown" years, I made countless choices that I'm sure my parents found both infuriating and ridiculous. They made absolute sense to me because, of course, that brick wall was going to move for me. As a result, I have had my share of bumps and bruises. So do you, so will your children. Just remember, we survived, so will they.

OLD STANDARDS

These are the sayings that go back for generations. No one actually knows who started them.

"If you like it, I love it!"
Virmell Hobson-Whitley

"You never miss your water until your well runs dry." **Jean C. Bellamy**

"Never mistreat the people you meet on your rise to the top. You may meet those same people on your way back down." **Louise Brown**

"This will hurt me more than it hurts you."
Gerald Tyler
I don't know anyone who believes a parent when they say this.

"If you don't go to church, you ain't going nowhere else." **Stephanie Credle**

"If you lay down with dogs, you get up with fleas." **Jackie Phillips**

"Why buy the cow if you can get the milk for free." **Louise Brown**

"There's always room for one more."
Leona LaPerriere

"God ain't through with me yet."
Octavia Jackson

"Every shut eye isn't asleep." **Gerri Staton**

"Things are not what they seem." **Ann Williams**

"Time will tell." **Latoya Corbin**

"If you dont't stand for something, You'll fall for anything." **Rosalind Tatum**

"If you don't have anything nice to say, don't say anything." **Ruthi Lee**

"Do unto others as you would have them do unto you. (The good old golden rule.)"
Vivian L. Washington

"Youth is wasted on the young." **Louise Brown**

"You can't miss what you never had."
Constance Griffin

"Many hands make the work light."
Rose M. Howard

"The early bird gets the worm." **Shari Wilson**

"Make sure to use the talents that you are blessed with."

In my opinion, my Aunt Virmell is a living breathing example of what GOD means when he tells us that we must discover and use the talents that he blesses us with. Several years ago, she had a stroke that confined her to a wheelchair.

Aunt Virmell

I remember getting a call from my father who told me that she had a stroke. My first thought was, "there is no way I'm going to sit around down here and wait to hear about what is going on. The next day I was in my car heading to New York. When I got to the hospital, a new fear gripped me as I rode the elevator to her floor. I wondered how much actual damage had been done by the stroke.

My Auntie is beautiful, vibrant, intelligent, and lively. I knew her as my fast-paced, trash talking, family member, friend, and mentor. The question in my mind was "Will the person I know still be there?" When I got to her room, I prepared myself as best I could for whatever I faced and walked in. The first thing I said to her was "Auntie, if you wanted me to come home all you had to do was call and say Lori come home. I would have just come home. All this drama was totally unnecessary!" She looked over at me and laughed. At that moment I knew that my Auntie was still with me. We spent the rest of the afternoon talking, laughing, and catching up. Her speech had been affected but she repeated things as many times as were needed to make sure that I understood what she was saying to me.

Eventually, my Auntie moved into a nursing home. When I visit her, I don't expect to find her in her room. She could be anywhere in the building. She is just as vibrant and lively as always and she still talks trash. I know that she will be fashionably attired and coordinated from head to toe. Before her stroke, Aunt Virmell was a science teacher. I've always thought that I'd love to have a child in her class because she has the creativity and talent to engage her students.

Today my Auntie teaches bible study in the nursing home. When she heard about my experience with the Prayer of Jabez (detailed in the Faith chapter), she gave me the book on CD and handouts from her classes.

During one of my visits she told me that she believes that GOD wants her to use her gifts. During one of my visits she told me that she believes that GOD wants her to use her gifts and talents where she is until he decides to heal her. I think that she is absolutely right. Who knows how many souls will be saved as a result of her teaching gift.

My Aunt Virmell's momma saying heads up this chapter.

灵 感

js

Inspiration

INSPIRATIONS AND AFFIRMATIONS

Choose one of these to begin and end each day or make up your own.

"I am grateful. I am kind. I create what's on my mind. Perfect health...Prosperity... My world reflects the change in me."
© 2007 Socratic Parenting LLC.

My husband and I carry Tokens of Change (www.TokenofChange.com) with us every day to remind us to live each moment with these intentions. Every night before our seven-year-old goes to sleep, she puts her Token of Change on her forehead and recites the poem. We process most of what has happened that day and any worries for tomorrow through the framework of this affirmation. If you ask her what "perfect health" means, she'll tell you that her body knows how to heal itself when she takes care of it and gets a good night's sleep. If you ask her what "prosperity" means, she'll tell you, "We have everything we need and enough to share with others." We approach Life/the Universe/God with gratitude and all living things, including the earth, with kindness. She's creating a beautiful world for herself and all those around her!

Laurie Gray

ON THIS DAY I WILL

- Love myself the way GOD loves me.

- Forgive my own imperfections and those of others.

- Know exactly where my beauty lies.

- Be president of my own fan club.

- Trust myself.

- Seek advice from those who have gone before me.

- Reach out to someone I haven't spoken to in a long time.

- Begin my day with a prayer.

- Wake up with gratitude.

- Value, nurture or improve everything that GOD has blessed me with.

- Seek GOD's blessings for my enemies.

- Stand in a full length mirror and show myself some appreciation.

- Not allow myself to spew verbal venom at anyone.

- Do something that is good for me.

- Accept it when GOD grants me the desires of my heart.

- Forgive someone who has hurt me.

- Let go of emotional pain, but keep the lesson. **Jewel Diamond Taylor**

- Take off my superwoman cape and learn how to delegate and say "no" to unnecessary demands of my time, energy and money. **Jewel Diamond Taylor**

SUGGESTED READINGS AND WEBSITES

Average Girl Magazine
www.averagegirlmagazine.com

Breathe Again Magazine
www.breatheagainmagazine.com

Finding Your Beauty
www.findingyourbeauty.com

Jewel Diamond Taylor
www.donotgiveup.net

Motivational Gifts Survey
www.gifttest.org

**Nice Girls Don't
Change the World**
by Lynne Hybels
(*available at www.lynnehybels.com*)

**Ordinary Women...
Extraordinary Success**
by Dr. Cherie Carter-Scott et al.

Se7en Magazine
www.757pages.net

Sixth Mount Zion Baptist Temple
www.smzbt.org

The Courage to be Yourself
by Sue Patton Thoele

The Blessedness of Believing:
A devotional journey of life's lessons and
God's promises
by Linda Mose Meadows

Dream Girlz
www.ccvinc.org/dreamgirlz

Destiny International Christian Center
www.dicconline.com

The Power of Full Engagement
by Jim Loehr and Tony Schwartz

Failing Forward
by John Maxwell

Fearless
by Steve Chandler

Act Like a Lady, Think Like a Man
by Steve Harvey

The Kelly Company Professional Service
www.thekelly-company.com

Derricknyms
www.derrickhayes.com

Sandy Dumont
www.theimagearchitect.com

The Hot Momma Project
www.hotmommasproject.org

Prayer of Jabez
by Bruce Wilkinson

Shari Wilson
www.shariROCKS.com

THE SENSATIONAL SIX
and the world's best success coach:

JB Rattles
www.jbrattles.com

Lattitude 4 U college division lee@tlgrp.com
www.lattitudegroup.com

Life by Design, Coaching and Hypnotherapy
www.hypnocoachlisa.com

L. H. Development
www.findingyourbeauty.com

Vintage Body Spa
www.vintagebodyspa.com

Women Who Wow
www.womenwhowow.com

Sounds Yummy Pet Bakery
www.soundsyummypb.com

ABOUT THE AUTHOR

Lori M Hobson is a Counselor, Trainer and Motivational Speaker.

She received her Bachelor's Degree in Psychology from Norfolk State University. Her Master's degree is in Rehabilitation Counseling from Hunter College Ms. Hobson is a Senior Staff Counselor in the Norfolk State University Counseling Center. She is involved in training Peer Educators as well as developing and presenting educational programming in the residence halls and classrooms. Additionally, Ms. Hobson is Coordinator of Substance Abuse Services. As Coordinator, she represents Norfolk State with: The Virginia College Alcohol Leadership Council, The Virginia Tidewater Consortium for Higher Education's Substance Abuse Committee and The National Historically Black Colleges and Universities Substance Abuse Consortium.

Ms. Hobson's community connections include an active membership in Sixth Mount Zion Baptist Temple in Hampton, Va., where she is part of the women's ministry. She has also served as Chair of the Board of Directors for Serenity House Substance Abuse Recovery Program in Newport News, Va.

Recently, Ms. Hobson was selected for inclusion in the Manchester Who's Who Among Executives and Professionals. She has been published in "Promising Practices, Programs of Excellence at America's Colleges and Universities". She has also been nominated for Woman of the Year by the American Biographical Institute Board of International Research.

Ms. Hobson is one of six recent graduates of the Spartan Leadership Institute at Norfolk State University. Currently, she is pursuing her Doctorate in Organizational Leadership at Nova Southeastern University. Although she is a native New Yorker, Ms. Hobson currently lives in Hampton, Virginia.

Lori M. Hobson provides several exciting and interactive workshops for men and women. Among them are:

Finding Your Beauty
Emotional Intelligence
Intergenerational Communication
How to Communicate with the Woman/Man in
Your Life
I Met the Man/Woman of My Dreams and then
I Woke Up!

Ms. Hobson will also design presentations to fit the needs of your organization.

For additional information or
to book this vibrant speaker

Call 757-224-8589
Fax 757-325-6617
Email lhdevelop@yahoo.com or
lhobson@findingyourbeauty.com

www.findingyourbeauty.com

Finding your beauty

www.ingramcontent.com/pod-product-compliance
Lightning Source LLC
Chambersburg PA
CBHW031216270326
41931CB00006B/575